*Butterflies and other insects
of the Eastern
Caribbean*

Dedication
To Jacqui

Butterflies and other insects of the Eastern Caribbean

PETER D. STILING

MACMILLAN
CARIBBEAN

First published 1986

Published by *Macmillan Publishers Ltd*
London and Basingstoke
Associated companies and representatives in Accra,
Auckland, Delhi, Dublin, Gaborone, Hamburg, Harare,
Hong Kong, Kuala Lumpur, Lagos, Manzini, Melbourne,
Mexico City, Nairobi, New York, Singapore, Tokyo

ISBN 0-333-38962-X

Printed in Hong Kong

British Library Cataloguing in Publication Data
Stiling, Peter D.
  Butterflies and other insects of the Eastern
  Caribbean.
  1. Insects—Caribbean Area—Identification
  I. Title
  595.7091821   QL479.A1

ISBN 0-333-38962-X

Contents

List of colour plates

Front cover: Orange-barred Sulphur, *Phoebis philea*

All photographs were taken by the author.

Acknowledgements

I wish to thank the following friends for help in collecting material: Trevor Akan, Param Deoraj, Julian Duncan, John, Heather and Jean Hutton, and Professor J.S. Kenny.

Species identifications were greatly helped by the efforts of Graham Rotheray (Royal Scottish Museum), Steve Brooks, Mike Cox, David Goodger, Judith Marshall, Allan Watson and Mike Wilson (all of the British Museum Natural History Section).

Introduction

Insects have lived on earth for about 300 million years, compared with less than one million for man. During this time they have adapted to live in almost every type of habitat on earth except the ocean. The larvae of petroleum flies live in pools of oil around California oil wells; the 'short-circuit' beetle of the western United States bores into lead cables, some flies have even been found breeding in the medical school brine vats in which human cadavers are preserved. More commonly insects are phytophagous, feeding on plant roots, leaves, stems, sap or bark or are predators and parasites of those phytophagous species.

Of the one and a half million species of plants and animals known on earth, well over half are insects. There are nearly ten times more species of Lepidoptera alone (butterflies and moths) than all mammals and birds combined. Herbivorous ungulate mammals muster few more than 200 species; phytophagous insects number well over a third of a million. This book restricts itself to the insects inhabiting the Lesser Antillean chain, but even here the diversity is staggering; it would be hopeless to attempt to describe even a tenth of them. Instead coverage of the main types of families has been attempted. In a few groups where the species are better known, for example the butterflies, treatment goes beyond the familial level.

It is a well known fact that tropical regions support a far greater number of animal species than temperate regions. Suprisingly, although the West Indies lie wholly within the tropics they muster fewer species of insects than Continental Europe, for example 292 species of butterflies against about 390. Central America, on an equivalent latitude, has seven times as many butterflies. The explanation is that the Caribbean islands are volcanic in origin, each arising separately from the sea bed. The Caribbean fauna consists of 'samples', derived from the mainland, which over an immense period of time have suceeded in establishing themselves on the islands. Many insects fly and could easily be transported by high winds. The principal route of immigration was from Central America via Cuba

1

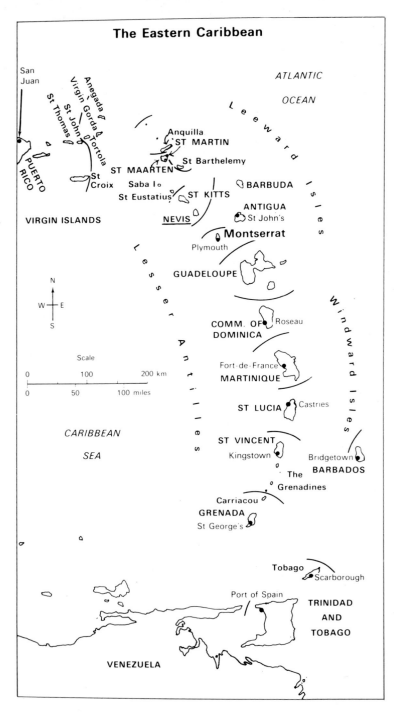

The Eastern Caribbean

ATLANTIC

OCEAN

San
Juan

Anegada
Virgin Gorda
St John
St Thomas
Tortola

L e e w a r d   I s l e s

Anguilla
ST MARTIN

ST MAARTEN
St Barthelemy

**PUERTO
RICO**

St
Croix

Saba I o
St Eustatius

ST KITTS

Ɋ **BARBUDA**

ANTIGUA
St John's

VIRGIN ISLANDS

NEVIS

Montserrat
Plymouth

L e s s e r

GUADELOUPE

N
W—E
S

A n t i l l e s

**COMM. OF
DOMINICA**
Roseau

Scale

0   100   200 km

0   50   100 miles

Fort-de-France
MARTINIQUE

W i n d w a r d   I s l e s

ST LUCIA
Castries

CARIBBEAN

SEA

ST VINCENT
Kingstown

The
Grenadines

Bridgetown
BARBADOS

Carriacou
GRENADA
St George's

Tobago
Scarborough

Port of Spain
**TRINIDAD
AND
TOBAGO**

VENEZUELA

then in stepping-stone fashion over Hispaniola, Puerto Rico and finally into the Lesser Antilles. Some species arrived from South America via Trinidad and Tobago and into the Eastern Caribbean. Larger islands generally have greater varieties of habitats and support more species. This, coupled with the fact that most species emigrated from Central America via Cuba, means that the Greater Antilles support many more types of insect than other Caribbean Isles. Hispaniola, for example, has 151 species of butterfly alone, 41 of which are endemic. Dominica, in the Leeward Islands has only two. Similar trends are evident in other insect groups, so that a comprehenisve description of the total Caribbean fauna would take many volumes. This volume restricts itself to the more narrow confines of the Lesser Antillian chain in the Eastern Caribbean, arguably the most accessible region. The species described and illustrated are found from the Virgin Islands in the north, through the Leeward chain of Anguilla, St Kitts, Barbuda, Antigua, Montserrat, Guadeloupe, Dominica and Martinique, and into the Windward Islands, St Lucia, St Vincent, Barbados, Grenada and the Grenadines, Tobago and Trinidad, the last of which being eight miles (or thirteen kilometres) from South America, has a more mainland fauna.

Insect classification

Many of the showy insects such as butterflies, or the particularly destructive pests, have common names. Other common names refer to groups: 'beetles' for all 300 000 species of Coleoptra, 'leaf beetle' for all 25 000 species of beetle in the family Chrysomelidae, 'tortoise beetle' for about 3000 species in the subfamily Cassidinae of the family Chrysomelidae. But because there are so many other insects which are poorly known, we cannot rely solely on common names. In 1758, the Swedish scientist Carl Von Linne (Latin: *Carolus Linnaeus*) proposed a binomial nomenclature for all organisms. This system provides two words which, when used conjointly, form the Latin or scientific name of each species. Formalised in the early 1900's this system has been in use ever since. Although it would be difficult to give each species a common name, Linne's system provided that each organism could be recognised by a unique name. The last name is the specific or species name, which is preceded by a generic or genus name. Groups of similar genera are grouped into families, eg, Carabidae, the ground or carabid beetles. Familial names, which often give rise to common names by the simple deletion of the last two letters, are here placed in parenthesis after common names. Similar families are grouped into orders such as

3

the grouping of all butterflies and moths into the Lepidoptera. Families may then be grouped together in classes, of which the class Insecta is one. Other animal classes include Mammalia (the mammals) and Aves (the birds). Finally within the animal kingdom, similar classes are grouped together into phyla (singular = phylum). Insects form part of the arthropod phylum together with non-insects such as spiders and crabs. Man belongs to the phylum Chordata.

This book considers insects, members of that class with six legs and usually two pairs of wings, one pair sometimes being reduced to halteres (see Diptera). Latterly, some common non-insect 'creepy crawlies' are considered. These include the centipedes (class Chilopoda), millipedes (class Diplopoda), and the spiders and scorpions (class Arachnida), all non-insects but united under the banner of the arthropod phylum together with crustaceans.

It is worth noting that the names 'fly' and 'bug' are often used for insects in more than one order. When 'fly' is written separately (eg, horse fly, hover fly), that insect belongs to the Diptera. When written together with a descriptive word (eg, dragonfly), the insect is in some other order. This rule also applies to the bugs.

Insect anatomy and life cycles

Compared with ourselves, insects are peculiarly constructed animals. They might be said to be inside out because the skeleton, or cuticle, is on the outside and is called an ectoskeleton. This ectoskeleton is inheritantly stronger than our endoskeleton. A hollow cylinder is

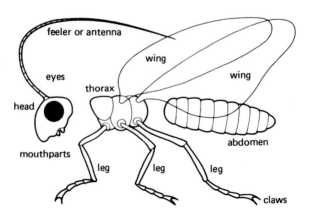

The main parts of a typical insect

stronger, sometimes much stronger, than a solid cylinder made of the same amount of material. The area of an ectoskeleton on which muscles can be attached is much greater than that of an endoskeleton, and this permits more advantageous placement of the muscles with respect to their leverages. This tough external armour is a great protector and this is perhaps why beetles, its chief exponents, are so abundant, being the most speciose order in the world and accounting for a third of all insects.

Insects might also be said to be upside-down because the nerve cord extends along the lower side of the body and the heart lies above the alimentary canal. They have no lungs but breathe through a number of tiny holes in the body wall, spiracles, air diffusing directly to the body tissues through many tiny branching tracheoles. Since insect blood is not involved in oxygen transport it has little haemoglobin: squashed insects do not look red. Gases can diffuse easily only over short distances, and once the diffusion distance from air to cells goes above a few millimetres the process becomes very slow. It is this which limits the size of an insect. Few species have diameters of much over one and a half centimetres; they simply could not obtain sufficient oxygen to survive. Diffusion distances of gases increase with temperature so that in a tropical temperature of 30°C (or 85°F) the rate of diffusion would be about fifteen per cent greater than at a temperate 10°C (or 50°F). This may account for the largest insects being tropical species.

Small size can be both a blessing and a handicap. It usually means a short life span, and more generations per year, providing greater opportunity for mutations and evolutionary change. On the other hand as a body decreases in size, the ratio of surface to volume increases and this increases the likelihood of water loss by evaporation. The impervious cuticle cuts down much of this loss but must be shed periodically to permit any growth. Small size also means less weight and thus increases the protective power of the skeleton. Flying insects can crash into obstacles with a force that would completely wreck a vertebrate, and take off again unharmed.

The insects are the only invertebrates with wings, and these have a different evolutionary history from the wings of vertebrates. Bird and bat wings are modifications of limbs but those of insects are additional to their limbs, and thus can be likened to the wings of the mythical flying horse, Pegasus. Wings allow insects to colonise the most temporary habitat, such as a rain-filled pool, yet leave when conditions again become unfavourable, and the pool dries out.

Insects are cold blooded, that is their body temperature follows very closely the external temperature to which they are exposed. In consequence, for many diurnal species, the ardent entomologist need not rise with the dawn chorus, he can relax in bed until the sun has sufficiently warmed his insects into activity.

In the nature of their development and life cycle, insects run the gamut from the very simple to the complex and amazing. From eggs, many undergo little change as they develop, the young hatchlings or 'first instars' being miniature adults. At each of about five moults, these little replicas become even more like their parents, gradually aquiring wings. Grasshoppers, mantids, cockroaches, termites and homopterans develop in this way. The vast majority, however, undergo in their development rather remarkable changes both in appearance and in habits. In butterflies an egg hatches into a worm-like caterpillar which eats ravenously, shedding its skin periodically as it grows. Finally, it moults into a pupa or chrysalis, hung like a ham in a meat shop, from which a beautiful winged butterfly emerges. If a mammal developed from a work-like grub it would be fantastic, yet the majority of insects have life cycles like that of a butterfly. A fly develops from a maggot, a beetle from a grub, and a bee, wasp or ant from a maggot-like grub. When these insects become adult they stop growing (and sometimes feeding); a little fly does not grow into a bigger one. These grubs or larvae often live and feed in habitats very different from the adults. Thus many beetles develop as root feeders, and many flies are scavengers in rubbish or detritus.

Insect and man

In relation to man, insects may be classified into two general groups: beneficial and injurious. Most people are more aware of the injurious group, yet the benefits that accrue from insects outweigh the harm they do.

Without insects the whole fabric of human society would change. In the United States, available figures suggest that insects are worth at least $5 billion annually. The largest fraction of this, $4½ billion, is due to the pollinating services of insects, chiefly bees, but also some flies and moths. Without them we would have few vegetables or fruits, little clover and hence less beef, mutton and wool, no cotton, no coffee, no tobacco, no chocolate and very few flowers.

Besides this vital service of pollination, insects provide us directly with honey, beeswax, and many other commercial products. The silk industry, world production of between 30 and 40 million kilograms annually, depends on the silkmoth, *Bombyx mori* and from scale insects (Homoptera) shellac and cochineal dyes are produced. Insects are the sole or major food item for many birds and fish. They also have aesthetic value, artists, milliners and designers making use of their beauty. Last but not least, parasitic and predaceous insects are important in keeping the numbers of other pest species down. The reproductive rate of insects is phenomenal. Unchecked *Drosophila* fruit flies can produce 100 eggs per generation and 25 generations a year. At the end of a year if all the flies of just the final generation were alive there would be about 10^{41}, enough, if packed 60 to a cubic centimetre, to form a ball of flies 150 million kilometres in diameter, or a ball extending nearly to the sun. That we are not knee deep in flies is due largely to beneficial insect predators and parasites.

Paramount among the injurious insects are those that attack important crops and those that transmit disease to humans and livestock. At least fifteen per cent of the world's food supply is destroyed annually by insects; the annual losses in the United States due to insect pests has been estimated at about $3½ billion annually. Although this is less than the benefits derived, the good is often less evident that the harm. About 16 000 labourers died of yellow fever during the construction of the Panama canal and work had to be postponed for several years until the disease could be controlled. In the Caribbean especially, memories of mosquito bites linger longer than visions of a beautiful butterfly.

The most noticeable damage to crops is that caused by chewing insects such as beetles, grasshoppers and Lepidoptera larvae. Often this damage is cosmetic and has little appreciable effect on yields. Cosmetic damage to fruits, however, cannot be tolerated. Even a single maggot in an apple is enough to put the consumer off. Perhaps more important as pests are the sap-sucking Homoptera which transmit lethal plant diseases. Over 200 plant diseases, three quarters of them viruses, have been shown to have insect carriers. Even low levels of pests are sufficient to transmit these diseases.

Of the insects attacking man and animals, the bites and stings of venomous species and the disturbance caused by parasitic insects may be severe but rarely fatal, but many insect borne diseases have high mortality rates. Insects act as agents in the transmission of disease in two general ways; as mechanical carriers or as biological carriers. Mechanical carriers such as house flies simply pick up pathogens on their feet and transfer them to food material. Typhoid, cholera and dysentry are transmitted in this way. In biological carriers the insect acts as a host in the life cycle of the pathogen, the germs living and multiplying within the insect's body prior to infecting other vertebrate hosts. Biological carriers are chiefly the bloodsucking Diptera and Hemiptera. Diseases spread in this way include malaria, still the world's chief killer of people, yellow fever and dengue (mosquitos), sleeping sickness (tsetse flies), and Chaga's disease (assassin bugs).

Collection and preservation

Insects can be found practically everywhere and in the Caribbean practically at any time. Rain will reduce the aerial activity of many insects but the following sunshine will bring them out again. Butterflies in particular like to cavort in patches of sunlight just after a shower of rain. For collecting these and other fliers it is best to use a net. Nets for general collecting should be of open mesh so that an insect can be seen through it. Size depends on personal preference, but most have a handle about a metre long, a rim of diameter 30 centimetres and a bag about twice as long as the diameter of the rim. Heavy duty nets are made of muslin and may be passed over vegetation dislodging the insects feeding there. A few beats will dislodge an astonishing array of insects. Aspirators or pooters are useful devices for capturing very small insects. One of these consists of a corked vial with two pieces of tubing leading in. Suck on one and point the other at the insect; it will be drawn into the vial with the influx of air. Try to put a piece of gauze over the mouthpiece tubing so that insects will not be drawn into the mouth. Crepuscular species, particularly beetles, can safely be picked up by hand but can also be trapped by sinking a jam jar into the ground; the insects will blunder into it. Beetles and a wide array of other insects including mantids, cockroaches, leafhoppers and moths are easily collected at night when they are attracted to bright lights.

For permanent collections insects are best killed by ethyl acetate, an ingredient of nail polish, lethal to insects. This liquid is poured onto cotton wool in the bottom of a wide-mouthed killing jar. Insects can be transferred directly to the jar or the end of the net containing the insect can be introduced. Killing jars involving cyanide, carbon tetrachloride or chloroform are recommended only for professionals. Failing the availability of ethyl acetate, 15 minutes in a freezer will kill any insect, the refrigerator though will simply stun them. The freezer also has the advantage of keeping insects supple; dead insects left under normal conditions soon develop *rigor mortis*, as do most dead animals. Stiff insects can be 'relaxed' or brought back to suppleness by 24 hours on moist cotton wool in a tin or jar. For permanent display all hard-bodied insects can be pinned, preferably with a special black steel insect pin, since household pins are too thick and too short, and they will rust. Insects are usually pinned vertically through the body and the wings are spread out for display. Special insect setting boards are available, but a piece of cork or polystyrene is often sufficient. Paper strips held across the wings will hold them in position until the insect drys or sets, in about a day. To complete the display a collector should label his specimens with date and locality, optional data include collector's name, and specimen identification. This information is usually incorporated onto a small label inserted on the pin below the specimen.

Ironically insect collections are subject to attack by other insects such as dermestid beetles which will eat a specimen and reduce it to dust. To avoid this catastrophy store your collection in a cool dry place and put mothballs, napthalene flakes or paradichlorobenzene crystals in one corner of the box. This will kill any pests present and protect them from further attack. These substances are volatile, however, and collections should be checked periodically and the preservatives renewed.

1 Order Odonata: dragonflies and damselflies

This is an ancient order with fossils resembling dragonflies dating back 300 million years, some with wingspans of over a foot. About 5000 species range worldwide. The immature stages of dragonflies and damselflies are aquatic, living in streams and ponds and feeding generally on other insects. As a result the adults are usually found near water although they are strong fliers and can range many miles. They often fly in tandem, the male holding the female by the back of the head with the appendages at the end of his abdomen. Damselflies, *Argia* sp. (Figure 1) are usually more slender than dragonflies but the acid test to distinguish the two groups is that dragonflies extend their wings horizontally to the sides when at rest whilst damselflies hold them toward the rear vertically. The commonest types of dragonfly are the skimmers, *Orthemis ferruginea* (Figure 2), which are brightly coloured with bodies shorter than the wingspan, and the darners, *Brechmorhoga praecox* (Figure 3), also brightly coloured but with longer, more slender bodies. Adults are predaceous on other insects and attempt to bite when handled, but only the larger dragonflies can inflict a pinch; they do not sting.

Resembling dragonflies in appearance are antlions (Figure 4), which belong to the order Neuroptera, the net-veined insects. Adult antlions are feeble fliers and the larvae are voracious predators. Often called 'doodlebugs', the larvae construct cone shaped pits in sandy ground. Here they wait, at the bottom of the pit, for ants and other insects to fall in. If the insect struggles to get out, the sides of the pit will crumble or the antlion larva will flick sand at it. Soon the mandibles of the larva close about the victim and suck out the body fluids. Antlion pits are commonly clustered together in dry sandy soil. Other common Neuroptera include the delicate pale green lace-wings, important aphid predators.

1 Damselfly, *Argia* sp.

2 Red Skimmer, *Orthemis ferruginea*

3 Darner, *Brechmorhoga praecox*

4 Antlion

5   Short-horned grasshopper, *Schistocera* sp.

6   *Tropidacris dux*

2 Order Orthoptera: grasshoppers and crickets

This is a diverse order containing such related forms as praying mantises, cockroaches and stick insects as well as grasshoppers and crickets.

Grasshoppers and crickets are easily recognised by their long, powerfully muscled hind legs that they use for jumping. In some species the legs are rubbed against the wings to produce characteristic chirping noises. More commonly this noise is produced by simply rubbing the toughened wings together. Males generally do the singing and each species has a distinctive song, instrumental in getting the sexes together. Grasshoppers are plant feeders and can be quite destructive as they chew away on crop leaves. Grasshopper digestion is incomplete and they have hearty appetites, eating up to their own weight in food a day. They are also untidy feeders leaving ragged edges and strips of unconsumed leaf hanging down. In times of great abundance some short-horned grasshoppers, *Schistocera* sp. (Figure 5) change their colour patterns and form huge migrating swarms which ravage the land. These are locusts (from the Latin for grasshopper), and the migrating swarms are simply the gregarious phase of normally solitary grasshoppers. Short-horned grasshoppers (family Acrididae), get their name from their short horn-shaped antennae, which are usually less than half the length of the body. Some species such as the giant neotropical *Tropidacris dux* (Figure 6) can exceed 15 cm in length. Nymphs resemble adults but have small wing pads instead of fully developed wings. Long-horned grasshoppers have extremely long antennae which reach back over and often beyond the body. Males have flat round hearing organs called 'tympana' at the base of the front legs. Females are often recognised by flat, sword-like ovipositors. Most species are greenish, matching perfectly the leaves on which they feed and lay their eggs. So good is the camouflage that even leaf veins

7 Leaf-like tettigoniid grasshopper,   8 *Pycnopalpa bicordata* (Tettigoniidae)
Philophyllia guttulata

and fungus spots are mimicked on the wings. See Figures 7 and 8.

Crickets (family Gryllidae) (Figure 9) resemble long-horned grasshoppers (katydids) but have long conspicuous tails, or *cerci*, at the end of the abdomen. Crickets' songs are much higher pitched than those of grasshoppers, and their diet is much broader, many species being omnivores.

Cockroaches (family Blattidae) are best known as house pests but most are wild, living in tropical forests and feeding on organic debris. *Blaborous colosseus* (Figure 10) can be over 7 cm long.

The walkingsticks (family Phasmida) are masters of camouflage; they resemble sticks, twigs and amongst tropical species, often the leaves on which they feed. Walkingsticks, *Bostra* sp. (Figure 11) can emit protective chemicals from special glands located on the thorax. Sprayed into the eyes of birds or other predators it is an effective defence mechanism. Failing that, unlike most insects, stick insects are capable of regenerating lost limbs. Often very slender and small, some species, such as the giant *Diapherodes gigantea* from St Vincent, are up to 25 cm long. The longest insect in the world is the giant 33 cm stick insect of Indonesia.

9 Cricket

10 *Blaborous colosseus*

11 Walkingstick, *Bostra* sp.

12 Praying mantis, *Stagmatoptera septentrionalis*

13 Praying mantis, *Acanthops falcata*

Mantids (family Mantidae) are large insects, usually over 2 cm, with a most distinctive appearance. The front legs are armed with spines for grasping insect prey. The praying mantis (*Stagmatoptera septentrionalis*, Figure 12, and *Acanthops falcata*, Figure 13) wait patiently for their next meal with these legs together and upraised, in a prayerful pose, inspiring their name. The neck is so long that the mantid can 'look over its shoulder', a bizarre and unique feature even amongst the insects. These are voracious eaters of even the most armoured insects, indeed the female often devours the male while mating. Despite this alarming habit, a male mantis can still go through the mating process, even with its head removed.

3   Order Hemiptera: true bugs

Although the term 'bug' is applied to many kinds of insects, non-insects and even bacteria, technically it is appropriate only to this group of insects. The distinctive feature of this order is the structure of the front wings, the basal portions being leathery and thickened, the apical portion membranous. The hind wings are entirely membranous. The mouth parts are of the piercing and sucking kind, and the diet being either plant sap or the body juices of other animals, mainly insects. Small to medium sized insects, the predominant colours are browns, greens and black, often marked with red in predatory species.

Wheel bug   Reduvidae   *Arilus cristatus*   Figure 14

The reduvid or assassin bugs get their name from the way they attack and inflict sharp stabs on their victims, before the body fluids are sucked out. Other insects, especially caterpillars, are preferred prey but a careless human hand can also receive a nasty nip, and a few actually suck vertebrate blood, transmitting diseases. In South America, Chagas disease, which causes severe heart damage, is transmitted by reduvid bugs of the genera *Panstrongylus*, *Rhodnius* and *Triatoma*. *Arilus cristatus*, the wheel bug, is a widespread species which has a distinctive cog-like thorax.

Leaf footed bug   Coreidae   Figures 15 and 16
Leptoglossus balteatus, Diactor bilineatus

Leaf-footed bugs all suck plant juices and give off foul-smelling secretions when approached. Obviously unpalatable, they advertise their distastefulness with bright colours, the efficiency of which is increased by the dilations on the legs.

18

14 Wheel bug, *Arilus cristatus*

15 Leaf-footed bug, *Leptoglossus balteatus*

16 *Diactor bilineatus*

17 Stink bug, *Edessa meditabunda*

Stink bug Pentatomidae *Edessa meditabunda*   Figure 17

Both adults and nymphs possess large stink glands on their under-surface from which they can discharge copius amounts of foul-smelling (pear-drop like) fluid when disturbed. The stink presumably affords some protection from predators although there are many records of bugs being eaten by birds, and even primitive human tribes. Curiously enough, when enclosed in a jar, pentatomids can be asphyxiated by their own smell. Most stink bugs (or shield bugs as they are also called) feed on plant sap. Females often stand guard over their clutches of barrel shaped eggs, possibly as a defence against egg predators.

4 Order Homoptera: cicadas, leafhoppers and their allies

The Homoptera and Hemiptera are very similar in many respects and are grouped together by some authorities as the Hemiptera, with two sub orders the Homoptera and the Heteroptera (Hemiptera here). In the Homoptera all four wings are entirely membranous. Homoptera are all plant sap feeders with piercing and sucking mouthparts. Many are carriers of plant viruses and diseases, though the physical act of

18 Cicada

feeding can itself cause plants to wilt. Many people from colder climates must be familiar with greenfly or aphids yet these are less common in the tropics. Their relatives, however, are not. Infestations of wax-like scale insects or whitefly, and fluffy cotton-like mealy bugs are often visible on the underside of leaves. The production of wax is fairly common among the sedentary stages of many Homoptera and may offer some degree of protection against the weather or natural enemies, in a manner similar to the 'spittle-masses' of frothy plant sap produced by the related cercropids or spittle-bugs.

Cicada   Cicadidae   Figure 18

Each species of cicada has its own distinctive song, sung with a deafening gusto by the males by means of sound producing organs or tymbals on the abdomen. In an unusual reversal of roles it is the female who actively locates her zithering mate. To the human ear, cicadas are great ventriloquists, the sound appears to come from misleading directions. Perhaps this is not so surprising since ventriloquist literally means 'belly-speaker' which is what the cicada really is.

Some northern cicadas are famous for their 13 or 17 year life cycles spent underground feeding on roots. In the tropics such periodicity is lost though the empty nymphal skins may still often be seen on tree trunks, the larvae having finally emerged from the ground, the adult flying off to leave only an empty shell.

Leafhopper   Cicadellidae   Figure 19

Leafhoppers are very common jumping insects, small (2–15 mm) but often beautifully coloured. These tiny insects are abundant on the underside of vegetation, individual species often being associated with single host plants; trees, shrubs or grasses. As they suck plant sap, honeydew is secreted from the anus. Essentially filtered plant sap, this sweet liquid attracts ants, flies and wasps. Leafhoppers can be serious pests, transmitting plant viruses or by their intensive feeding causing 'hopperburn', a white stippling of the leaves where the sap has been extracted.

Treehopper   Membracidae   *Stegapsis viridis*   Figure 20

Closely related to leafhoppers, these sap feeders often exhibit bizarre shapes. The pronotum may extend far back over the thorax lending the insect the appearance of a thorn of the plant on which it rests.

23

19 Leafhopper

20 Treehopper, *Stegapsis viridis*

21 Alligator bug, *Laternaria laternaria*

Alligator bug   Superfamily Fulgoroidea   Figure 21
Laternaria laternaria

The superfamily Fulgoroidea (planthoppers) is the third group of small abundant, sap sucking Homoptera. Some tropical species, however, are quite large, like the alligator or lantern bug, *Laternaria laternaria*. This curious insect was at one time mistakenly thought to be luminous, hence its common name. The elongated head, probably a food reserve, has an uncanny resemblance to an alligator head. Some natives of South America believe this head to contain a deadly poison. Whether other large predators, such as monkeys, which are partial to other large Homoptera such as cicadas, are frightened by this appearance is not known.

5 Order Coleoptera: the beetles

Beetles are the most abundant in number of species of any group of organisms. Beetles and the entire plant kingdom have approximately the same number of species. There are more species of weevils (family Curculionidae) than there are types of bird in the world. Beetles include both the smallest insect (about 0.025 mm) and the largest (150 mm), equivalent to a large moth in size but much heavier. Despite the powerful mandibles of these large specimens, most can be easily handled and none sting.

Bessbug Passalidae   Figures 22 and 23

Bessbugs, also referred to as patent leather beetles or passalids, are some of the most common inhabitants of rotting logs where larvae and adults live in communal galleries. When disturbed, bessbugs make a squeaking sound by rubbing roughened areas under their wings across their backs. Despite their size and strong mandibles, passalids do not bite.

Tiger beetle Cicindelidae   Figure 24

Tiger beetles are medium sized beetles, often brightly coloured or metallic, found in hot, dry places. They are predacious on other insects and are very agile, running fast and frequently making short rapid flights. The larvae make vertical burrows in the soil, often near the seashore. Here the larvae lie with the head level with the ground, waiting to strike at any insects that come in range. Being firmly anchored in their tunnels, they are difficult to remove. Slowly inserting a grass stem can cause the larvae to bite. If withdrawn slowly, the stem may bring out with it a larva, still attached.

22   Bessbug, adult

23   Bessbug, larva

24 Tiger beetle

25 Carabid beetle, *Enceladus gigas*

26 Buprestid beetle, *Psiloptera variolosa*

Ground beetle Carabidae *Enceladus gigas* Figure 25

Ground beetles are commonly found under stones, logs, leaves and debris where they hide during the day. Venturing out mainly at night, nearly all are predaceous on other insects. Many are large, shiny black insects and some may give off disagreeable odours when handled. Amongst the smaller carabids, the bombardier beetle is able to eject a volatile liquid from the anus which vapourises on contact with the air into a tiny cloud of smoke. They are able to 'shoot' several times in succession, each with an audible report, before their ammunition is temporarily exhausted. The fluid is caustic, capable of raising a distinct blister on the skin, and is a means of protection.

Metallic wood-boring beetle Buprestidae Figure 26
Psiloptera variolosa

So beautiful are many metallic wood-boring beetles that the wing cases or elytra are used as jewellery. Adults fly quickly, often visiting flowers.

Larvae can be serious pests in tropical timbers, excavating large galleries in the wood. These are the longest living insects in the world, some of which remain in the larval stage for up to 30 years.

Click beetle Elateridae   Figures 27 and 28
Chalcolepidius porcatus, Pyrophorus pellucens

Click beetles get their name from the sharp clicking sound overturned beetles make when they flip themselves into the air. This acrobatic feat is accomplished by snapping a fingerlike spine on the underside of the thorax into a groove below the mesothorax. In other beetles this joint in the thorax is not flexible. If a click beetle is placed on its back on a smooth surface, being unable to right itself by means of its legs, it will bend its head and prothorax backwards so that only the extremities are touching the surface. With a sudden jerk the body is straightened out snapping the spine into the groove and propelling the beetle end over end into the air. If the beetle does not land right side up it will continue clicking until it does.

Members of the genus *Pyrophorus* are bioluminescent, a feature shared only with fireflies amongst the common insects. Two light producing organs are situated at the sides of the thorax. These light up

27 Click beetle, *Chalcolepidius porcatus*

28 *Pyrophorus pellucens*

during flight and also when the insect is disturbed at rest.

Held between thumb and forefinger in a darkened room, these beetles can supply enough light to enable one to read the print of a newspaper placed underneath. Tropical members are also sometimes caught for use as decorations at parties.

Fireflies Lampyridae   *Aspidosoma ignitum*   Figures 29 and 30

The name firefly is an unfortunate one since these insects are really beetles. The segments near the end of the abdomen produce light so that these evening fliers appear to have tail lights. Even in the day, when not glowing, these luminous segments can be recognised by their yellowish-green colour. The light emitted is unique in being cold; nearly 100% of the energy given off appears as light. (In an electric light bulb only 10% of the energy is light, the other 90% is given off as heat.) The light is produced by the oxidation of a substance called luciferin, which is produced in photogenic organs. (The word 'photogenic' means light producing and does not strictly refer to film stars.) These organs have a rich tracheal supply and the insects control the emission of light by controlling the air supply to the organs. The flashing of fireflies is probably a mating response, each species having a

29 Firefly, *Aspidosoma ignitum*, front view

30 Firefly, back view showing photogenic organ

31 The Harlequin beetle, *Acrocinus longimanus*

characteristic flashing pattern. Males can sometimes be duped, however, by predaceous females who mimic the flashing patterns of other species then eat the incoming males. The luminescence may also serve as a warning sign since the insects are distasteful and emit light during the day when touched. The larvae are also luminous and feed on small animals under ground debris. In some parts of the tropics, children introduce adult fireflies under mosquito nets to produce their own fascinating light show, though the light of the luminescent click beetles is stronger.

Long-horned beetles Cerambycidae   Figures 31 and 32
Acrocinus longimanus, Lagochirus araneiformis

Long-horned beetles often are admired for their beautiful colours and long antennae, which can be three times as long as the body. Both larvae and adults feed on the wood of dead or dying trees and can be very destructive. Wood is not a very nutritious diet and consequently larval tunnels are quite extensive.

32 *Lagochirus araneiformis* (Cerambycidae)

33 Tortoise beetle (Chrysomelidae)

34 The Hercules beetle, *Dynastes hercules*, male and, below, female

35 Scarab beetle, Rutelinae

Leef beetle Chrysomelidae Figure 33

Leaf beetles are usually small and convex but have bright metallic colours that glisten in the sun. Some species, often referred to as tortoise beetles, which resemble ladybird beetles in shape, are brilliantly coloured in life with golden or silver markings, but these colours may fade after death. In common with many other phytophages, chrysomelids leave characteristic evidence of their feeding. Some create many small round holes as if the leaf had been peppered with a shot gun. Others stand in one place and turn slowly as they feed, creating sickle shaped holes.

Scarab beetle Scarabaeidae Rutelinae Figures 34 and 35

Scarabs are stout beetles which feed on a variety of materials including plant roots and foliage. Many also develop as larvae inside balls of dung rolled by the adult females as a food provision for their young.

In Ancient Egypt related scarabs were associated with rebirth.

Scarabs, both real ones and clay images, were placed on mummies in tombs.

The large horns on the males of some species are not just ornamental but are used in close combat in the battle over possession of a female. The Hercules beetle is the largest known, though not the heaviest, a distinction which belongs to the Goliath beetles of Equatorial Africa.

Weevil Curculionidae   Figure 36

The characteristic feature of weevils is the head which is elongated into a slender downcurved beak or snout with elbowed antennae partway down, and mandibles at the tip. All members of this speciose group feed on plants, the females boring into fruit, seeds and stems to lay eggs.

6 Order Diptera: the flies

The distinguishing feature of flies is that they each have only one pair of wings, the second pair having been modified to short balancing sensory organs called halteres, which function in the same manner as a gyroscope. Most other aerial insects have two pairs of wings. Flies of one kind or another are found almost everywhere. Many of the primitive species are aquatic in the larval stage, while their adults, such as mosquitoes, tend to be bloodsuckers. It is usually only the females which have this annoying habit, they need the valuable protein to mature the eggs; males are innocuous nectar feeders. Other annoying flies include the black fly which bites viciously, particularly near the larval breeding grounds in streams, tabanids (horse flies and deer flies) and the biting midges (punkies or 'no-see-ums') whose mouthparts must be among the bluntest in the world: these tiny insects can give an excruciating bite. Midges have the fastest wing beat of any insect with a recorded rate of 100 000 beats per minute. Again the larvae are aquatic or semi-aquatic and commonly infest beaches to mar the tropical paradise. Whilst other animals such as birds, mammals and even other insects may be the normal hosts, man is also now a favoured target. Besides the mere distraction of these bites, Diptera, through their bloodsucking habits are probably the most important vectors of disease. Yet not all species are 'vampires', others infest carrion, dung and decaying matter and are an integral part of the detritus cycle. Some are also important parasites of other insects and are useful in pest control.

Horse fly Tabanidae   Figure 37

These stout, broad headed flies have bulging, often brightly coloured eyes, although the physiological significance of these colours, which disappear after death, is unknown. Both the larger tabanids, horse flies, and smaller ones, deer flies, feed on mammalian blood, though only the females bite. The males feed on flowers.

Flight is silent and these flies can land stealthily on exposed skin which they then slice open with bladelike mouthparts and suck up the blood. The wound may continue to bleed for several minutes because the fly's saliva contains an anticoagulant that prevents clotting. As with many bloodsuckers it is this that causes irritation. Notwithstanding the risk of disease, an animal may be severely debilitated by blood loss alone if it is severely attacked.

Robber fly   Asilidae   Figure 38

These are common, swift-flying predators, of medium size. They are usually bristly or hairy and the eyes, like those of so many predators, are prominent. Adults do not actively chase their prey in the manner of dragonflies, but usually sit in wait on foliage, often in strong sunlight, ambushing passing insects. Their mouthparts are very strong, capable of piercing the horny shells of beetles and wasps, and can inflict a painful bite if mishandled. The larvae, which live in ground debris, also feed on other insects.

37 Horse fly *Tabanus* sp.   **38** Robber fly

Long legged fly   Dolichopodidae   Figure 39

These are small flies, less than 10 mm long, but conspicuous by their bright metallic green or copper colouration. The adults are common in damp woods and fields where they may be seen running over the foliage in pursuit of small insect prey. Larvae too are predatory in damp soil, rotting wood or water. Males have unusually large genitalia which are folded underneath the abdomen. They perform elaborate mating dances in front of females, often exhibiting fans of black and white scales on the legs. Unlike many other courting insects the male fly is in no danger of being eaten by the female because her mouthparts are too small.

Hover fly   Syrphidae   Figure 40

One of the most attractive families of Diptera is the Syrphidae or hover fly family. Many are brightly coloured and all are superb aerial acrobats, their flying ability being unsurpassed in the animal world. They commonly hover motionless above flowers or in sunlit glades; stretch your arm out and they may hover above that too, maintaining their station perfectly by delicately hovering in any direction. Adults

39   Dolichopodid fly   **40**   Hover fly

feed on nectar and many mimic the warning colouration of wasps, having black and yellow striped abdomens. Yet syrphids are completely harmless and cannot sting. The larvae, frequently called maggots in common with other fly larvae, occupy a variety of habitats. The rat-tailed maggots are scavengers in polluted water, and develop long snorkel-like tubes, at the tip of the abdomen, through which they breathe. The majority of species are predators on aphids which they suck dry, consuming up to 1000 before they develop completely. Since aphids are, as a rule, more abundant in temperate climes, so too are hover flies.

7 Order Hymenoptera: wasps, ants and bees

Wasps, ants and bees are well known for their stings, social structure and nest building. Many are phytophagous but even more are parasitic and develop as larvae inside other insects. They are therefore valuable as insect pest control agents and many are also beneficial as flower pollinators.

Ichneumon wasp Ichneumonidae *Enicospilus* sp.   Figure 41

This is a very large family of parasitic wasps, members of which are

41 Ichneumon wasp, *Enicospilus* sp.

often attracted to lights at night. Adults drink nectar and water but lay their eggs on, in or near other insects, especially larvae, which are then consumed. The thread-like ovipositor, used to lay the eggs, is strong enough to pierce wood to parasitise wood boring larvae. Yet most species do not sting. Many parasites may develop in a single host individual depending on the size of the host and the size of the parasite. There are very few insects that are not liable to attack by at least one species of parasite, and often by more than one.

Velvet ant Mutillidae   Figure 42

Despite their name, velvet ants are really densely hairy wasps. Males are fully winged but females lack wings and can frequently be encountered wandering along on the ground. Larvae are parasitic, developing mainly inside the nests of other ground-dwelling bees or wasps. Females are brightly coloured – red, yellow or orange – and can sting painfully.

43   Spider wasp, *Pepsis* sp.

Spider wasp   Pompilidae   *Pepsis* sp.   Figure 43

These long-legged, medium to large-sized wasps are generally glossy
blue black in colour and can often be seen running on the ground
nervously flicking their dark wings. They are in search of spiders
which they paralyse and drag back to underground nests where the
eggs are laid on their newly provisioned food. If the prey were killed
before being put in the burrow, it would soon desiccate and be of little
food value to the developing wasps. Paralysis induced by the sting
ensures the food supply will be fresh. The number of spiders placed in
the nest depends largely on their size. Some tropical *Pepsis* species are
among the largest known wasps, with a wing span of nearly three
inches (8 cm). These often fill their nests with tarantulas, which,
though formidable, are no match for the quick moving wasps. Under-
standably the larger spider wasps can deliver painful stings.

44 Sphecid wasp, *Sceliphron figulus*

45 *Polistes canadensis* (Vespidae) and nest

46 Killer bee

Sphecid wasp Sphecidae *Sceliphron figulus* Figure 44

Sphecid wasps may be dark brown or black, or more often black and yellow with a very attenuated waist. This large group exhibits a variety of life styles. Many species dig nests in sandy areas and provision them with bugs, crickets and grasshoppers, sometimes re-opening the burrow to introduce fresh provisions and re-sealing it, using a small pebble held between the mandibles to tamp down the earth. Alternatively they may use their heads for this purpose. This is in contrast to spider wasps which use their abdomens for closing the burrow.

Other sphecids build mud cells on the side of walls, buildings and rocks, provisioning them with spiders. Such structures may be fairly long and other cells are often constructed nearby so that an appearance of organ-pipes is achieved.

Paper wasp Vespidae *Polistes canadensis* Figure 45

Vespids are medium size wasps similar to sphecids in their striped or dark brown colouration but differing in their wings which fold back over the abdomen and appear pleated. The majority of vespids are also social, living in colonies, although a few are solitary and dig mud-lined tunnels for their larvae or construct cells of mud, such as the pot-shaped chambers of potter wasps. Generally though, vespids live in colonies; they lay their eggs in combs of cells made of paper, feed their young chewed-up insects and show some degree of social behaviour. Social organisation ranges from groups of cooperating females, as in the paper wasps, to the caste system of yellow jackets and hornets in which there is a single fertile queen and a large population of smaller female workers that do not lay eggs. All of these sting painfully.

Killer bee Apidae Figure 46

Bees form a large group of insects specialised for feeding from flowers. When a bee visits a flower, pollen sticks to the hair. Most female bees have special pollen baskets or brushes, on the hind legs, which are used to brush the body and collect the pollen. Most bees are solitary and store the pollen and honey (transformed nectar) in underground tunnels of brood cells for larvae. Honey bees and bumble bees are social, living in colonies consisting of a fertile queen, sterile female workers and males, or drones. They are the only bees to produce and store honey. The combs of bees are made, not of chewed paper-like

45

material as those of the wasps, but of wax, a secretion produced from the digestion of honey or sugar. It has been shown mathematically that the hexagonal cell of the honey-bee is the most efficient for the storage of the greatest possible amount of honey with the least possible consumption of wax. Bees can sting, though usually only in defence of the colony. A bee can sting only once since the sting (a modified ovipositor) is barb-covered and withdrawal fatally ruptures the abdomen. Wasp stings on the other hand are not barbed and, unfortunately, can be used repeatedly.

Honey bees (*Apis mellifera*) have been taken all over the world. The African honey bee is more aggressive than other varieties and has a greater tendancy to sting. A breeding programme was established in South America involving ordinary honey bees and introduced African varieties. In 1957, twenty-six swarms of Africanised honey bees escaped from a laboratory in Sao Paulo and have been mating with docile European varieties and expanding their range ever since. They have recently been found in Trinidad and Tobago; how long will it be before the so-called killer bees turn up on the other islands?

Euglossine bee   Euglossidae   Figure 47

The so-called long-tongued bees are brilliant metallic green or blue non-social bees that are mainly neotropical in distribution. These solitary bees exercise the same degree of parental care as many solitary wasps, in that they construct cells for them, but these are provisioned with honey and pollen instead of insects and spiders, for no bees are carnivorous. Cells are constructed in many nooks and crannies including keyholes which may become so gummed up that it is impossible to turn the key.

Leaf-cutting parasol ant   Formicidae   Figure 48

Ants comprise a vast single family, the Formicidae, some members of which are familiar to all of us. As with many animals, the number of species increases with decreasing latitude so that the tropics are particularly rich in ants. All ants are social insects though there is a wide range in the complexity of their behaviour. Some are slave-makers and raid the nests of others to steal the larvae and raise them as slaves. Some are truly parasitic on other colonies. Driver ants of Africa and Army ants of South America have no fixed colonies but transport queen and larvae through the forest each day as they search for food, bivouacing at night. Powerful soldier ants with enlarged mandibles patrol the edges of foraging columns and can give nasty

47 Euglossine bee

48 Leaf-cutting ant, and,
below, the result of its activity

bites. Soldiers are modified worker ants, other castes being the king, queen and minor sterile workers. Ants are comparatively long-lived, workers surviving often for two years and the queen for several.

No special cells are constructed for larvae in ant nests; they are shifted about by workers as the occasion demands.

Amongst the more primitive ants are the ponerines, large black ants which scavenge for food. All ants are fond of sweet substances and will suck from the extra-floral nectaries of certain plants. However, the main source of sugar is honeydew, the liquid excreta of various Homoptera, particularly aphids, coccids and membracids. The ants will farm or stroke to induce excretion, whilst actively attacking other insects which alight close to their 'cows' and may disturb them.

The gardeners of the ant world are the leaf-cutters, common on most islands and highly visible slicing segments from leaves and transporting them aloft, like parasols, back to the nest. The leaves are not eaten but are chewed up as food for a fungus which is cultivated in underground chambers. It is this fungus which forms the food of leaf-cutting ants. Like most Hymenoptera, many ants can sting or bite and should be handled with respect. The poison is a mixture of several toxic ingredients, mainly proteins, and its potency has little to do with the size of the insect. Only the Formicinae family of ants secretes formic acid, and this is squirted from the anus, often onto wounds caused by biting.

8 Order Isoptera: termites

The main difference between termites and the Hymenoptera is that the former are primitive insects with a gradual metamorphosis; there is no helpless larval stage. Males and females are produced in equal numbers and are represented in all castes. However, there is no strict worker caste, the work of the colony is performed by young soldiers and reproductives. Eggs must be fertilised to develop so the king is as long-lived as the queen. Some termites live entirely on the ground, building termite mounds or termitaria, passing unnoticed. Most Caribbean

49 Termite nest

termites construct large spherical nests on tree trunks or plant stems (Figure 49). They feed on wood but are reluctant to forage in sunlight, so they construct enclosed tunnels of wood pulp leading from their nests to the ground in order to move around in darkness. Any damage to these tunnels is soon repaired.

Wood, particularly cellulose, is a difficult substance to digest and termites have intestinal protozoa which perform the conversion to glucose for them.

Soldier termites are usually more strongly differentiated than those of ants, being strongly pigmented and with large heads. Some have powerful mandibles, but in the common *Nasutitermes*, the 'Nasute' soldier has a retort-shaped head which contains a gland capable of emitting a fluid highly repellent to ants, their hereditary enemies. Often, as in many human states, the soldiers outnumber the workers. Why this should be so is not clear.

9 Order Lepidoptera: the butterflies

Lepidoptera are rightly considered to be among the most beautiful of creatures. Some large, tropical butterflies are very valuable and may be sold for thousands of dollars. The bright colours exist usually to warn would-be predators of a bad taste or poison in the body. The best way to obtain perfect specimens is to rear them from caterpillars, but even then the wings often remain crumpled on emergence from the chrysalis and do not fully expand to their proper shape.

Butterflies generally fly in the day and moths at night, when many are attracted to lights. There are, however, several families of fast day-flying moths that closely resemble the skipper butterflies. One of the most reliable ways to tell butterflies and moths apart is by their antennae: those of moths are generally feather-like or thread-like, those of butterflies always have club shaped tips.

Most butterflies and moths live less than a few months, just long enough to mate and lay eggs. They obtain their energy from nectar, sucked from flowers through a long coiled tube known as a proboscis. Some do not feed at all as adults, and food is gathered only in the larval or caterpillar stage. Many caterpillars are leaf eaters, others infest plant stems or feed on roots whilst still others are leaf miners, creating thin white lines or blister-like blotches between the surfaces of a leaf. Caterpillars are often host specific, feeding only on one particular type of plant; indeed the distribution patterns of certain Lepidoptera are limited by food plant availability.

There are over 180 000 described species of Lepidoptera in the world ranging from the large, with 15 cm wing span, to the tiny, 2 mm across. Small moths, in particular, are very abundant and are collectively referred to as the Microlepidoptera. Specific feeding patterns of the larvae, such as leaf mining, obviously restrict larval size and this is reflected in the size of the adult.

50 Orion, *Historis osius*

51 The Cracker, *Hamadryas feronia*

Many are dull and uninteresting, brown being the predominent colour, but members of groups such as the Pyralidae, Noctuidae and Tortricidae, are economically important crop pests and should not be ignored. Lepidopteran larvae are among the most important pests of the world, yet the adults are often valuable plant pollinators. Adults of some of the larger species are also of great beauty and their biology is among the best known amongst the insects. Details of distribution ranges, food plants and larval characteristics of many spectacular species are known and these have been included in the following section.

It is a common observation that many nocturnal insects such as moths are attracted to lights. Normally these insects fly in straight lines, navigating by the parallel rays of the Moon. The rays of artificial lights are not parallel and so the moths' efforts to fly at a constant angle to the light causes them to move in ever decreasing circles into the light, or to come to rest where they are equally illuminated from both sides.

Nymphalidae: Fritillaries, etc

There is no single morphological character by which to distinguish this large and cosmopolitan family. Features common to the group include fairly well developed antennae with club-like tips, and forelegs that are either absent or brush-like, useless for walking. Nymphalids occupy areas from the equator to the high temperate zones.

Orion   *Historis osius*   Figure 50

The wings have velvety dark brown uppersides and cryptically coloured undersides. At rest with the wings folded, the Orion blends into the background which is often tree bark. Ranging from southern North America to Argentina, it is a strong flyer and is found on all the islands. The light green caterpillar is 75 mm long when fully grown, with light brown transverse markings and black and white spines. The head is white with short black spikey horns. It feeds on *Cecropia peltata* trees.

The Cracker   *Hamadryas feronia*   Figure 51

The species of the genus *Hamadryas* are called Crackers because this is the noise they make in flight. How this sound is produced is not known. This is another South American species from Brazil and Equador ranging up through Trinidad to St Lucia and possibly further. The colour is mottled bluish-grey, identical in both sexes. The caterpillar is grey-green with many spines and feeds on *Dalechampia*, a Euphorbiaceae.

Red Rim   *Biblis hyperia*   Figure 52

A fairly slow flier frequenting open ground, feeding often on rotting fruit but also settling, with open wings, on green vegetation. The caterpillar feeds on Pine Nettle, *Tragia volubilis* and is spiny and grey-brown with small green warts. The upperside of the adult butterfly is velvety dark brown with a broad red band running along the border of the hindwing. Widespread throughout the lesser Antilles, and Northern South America.

Malachite   *Siproeta stelenes*   Figure 53

This is a beautiful butterfly with vivid green in large blotches and bands on a dark brown background. A solitary flier throughout the Lesser Antilles, South and Central America, it only congregates in numbers around rotting fruit. The velvety black caterpillar is about 40 mm long when full grown with pink prolegs, a shiny head with horns, and several spiny warts on the thoracic and last abdominal

52   Red Rim, *Biblis hyperia*

53 Malachite, *Siproeta stelenes*

54 Red Anartia, *Anartia amathea*

55 White Peacock, *Anartia jatrophae*

56 St Lucia Mestra, *Mestra canna*

segments. It feeds on *Blechum brownei* another common member of the Acanthaceae.

Red Anartia   *Anartia amathea*   Figure 54

Red and black with a sprinkling of white spots on the forewing. The red of the male is deep and vivid. In the female it shows a brownish pallor. Distributed throughout the Lesser Antilles this species becomes more common moving southwards towards South America. In Trinidad the 'Coolie', as it is locally known, is easily the most common butterfly. The caterpillar is black with stout black spines and feeds on species of Acanthaceae shrubs.

White Peacock   *Anartia jatrophae*   Figure 55

A common butterfly of open country, roadsides, beaches and wasteland, often in association with other species such as the Buckeye. On the wing all the year round in all of the islands, Brazil, Venezuela and the Guyanas. The upperside is light grey with six black dots. The

57 Caribbean Buckeye, *Junonia evarete*

caterpillar is black spotted with silver, similar to that of the Buckeye, and feeds on Water Hyssop, *Bacopa monniera.*

St Lucia Mestra   *Mestra canna*   Figure 56

Confined to the Windward Islands: Dominica, St Lucia, St Vincent, Barbados, Grenada, Trinidad and Tobago; also present in northern South America. A fairly common but drab yellow grey species with light whitish grey patches. A slow flier, settling on flowers bordering hill tracks and roadsides.

Caribbean Buckeye   *Junonia evarete*   Figure 57

The basic colour of this butterfly is dark brown with lighter brown shadings on the forewing and margin of hindwing. The wing spots have pupils of violet. A common species with a fast, deceptive flight, settling often on dry, open ground. Wide ranging throughout the Caribbean and also Central and South America. The caterpillar is black, with minute white dots and five rows of black or yellow

58 Southern Dagger Tail, *Marpesia petreus*

59 The Mimic, *Hypolimnas misippus*

branching spines. Fairly wide range of larval food plants including *Stachytarpheta* (Blue Vervain), *Lippia,* and *Valerianoides.*

Southern Dagger Tail   *Marpesia petreus*   Figure 58

Confined to the Lesser Antilles, Central and South America, this species, sometimes referred to as the Tailed Flambeau, is difficult to distinguish from the Flambeau or Silver Spot. Upperside is bright orange-brown with three thin black transerve lines on each wing; the distinguishing feature is the prominent tails of the hind wings.

The Mimic   *Hypolimnas misippus*   Figure 59

Distributed worldwide, the females resemble varieties of the Old World *Danaus chrysippus* with colouration not dissimilar to *Danaus glippus,* the Queen. Males however, are velvety black with irridescent purple encircling large white spots. Caterpillars are gregarious, black with grey bands, spiny and with red heads.

The '89'   *Callicore aurelia*   Figure 60

A fairly small butterfly (wingspan 40 mm) the '89' is typically South American but is also fairly common in Trinidad and Tobago,

60 The '89', *Callicore aurelia,* side and top views

preferring elevated localities. Black with metallic sheen and two gold stripes on the forewing, the figures '89' are precisely designated to the underside of the wings, visible at rest.

Heliconiidae: Heliconias

A rather small family confined to the Neotropics, the tropics of the New World. Always brightly coloured and tending to alight with wings open, presenting a picture of breathtaking beauty. The head is often large with big eyes, thin antennae and slender body. Bad odour and taste to predators and a considerable element of mimicry to other noxious species. The caterpillars, all of which feed on Passifloracea, Passion Flowers, are generally conspicuously coloured with bare branched spines: one pair on the head, one pair on each thoracic segment and three spines on all other segments. Of the seven genera usually recognised, *Heliconius* is the largest in terms of species, though relatively few frequent the West Indies.

The Zebra *Heliconius charitonius*

Occurring from Montserrat northwards, through Antigua, St Kitts and the Virgin Islands, this unmistakable butterfly is black with numerous broad yellow stripes. The caterpillar is creamy white, each segment being encircled by three dark bands.

The Doris *Heliconius doris*   Figure 61

This species is trimorphic, that is it exists in three colour varieties. Individuals of either sex can exhibit red, green or blue colouration, in addition to the basic black pattern with yellow blotches. The differentiating colour occurs at the basal area of the lower wing. The most common variety is the red, illustrated here. Typically a South American species it also ranges into Trinidad.

The Small Blue Grecian *Heliconius sara*   Figure 62

An inhabitant of cool shaded forest undergrowth or the tracks and shady outskirts of forested areas. Another Trinidadian species easily confused with the Blue Grecian is *Heliconius wallacei*, which at 70 mm wing span, is 12 mm bigger in span than *Heliconius sara*.

61   The Doris, *Heliconius doris*

62   The Small Blue Grecian, *Heliconius sara*

63 The Postman, *Heliconius melpomene*

64 Flambeau, *Dryas iulia*

65   Silver Spot, *Dione juno*

The Postman   *Heliconius melpomene*   Figure 63

Very dark brown with a broad red central forewing band. Common only in Trinidad and Tobago, but very frequent there in forested areas and shaded tracks. With a wingspan of over 70 mm it is very similar to but slightly larger than its close relative, *Heliconius erato* (wingspan less than 60 mm).

The Flambeau   *Dryas iulia*   Figure 64

A wide-ranging golden orange butterfly, common throughout the Caribbean with each island having its own endemic subspecies, each of which is nevertheless instantly recognisable as a Flambeau. This indicates an extreme sedentary habit, with little tendancy towards migration. A common species also in the Southern USA and South America. A butterfly of the lowlands with a dark and very spiny caterpillar. The closely related Silver Spot, *Dione juno* (Plate 65) occurs in very similar habitats, such as lowland flower gardens, from Martinique southwards into South America. It is distinguished by the bright silver spots on the underside which give the butterfly its common name. Caterpillars are reddish brown with six rows of spines; they feed gregariously on passion flowers, *Passiflora* sp. as do Flambeau caterpillars.

The Gulf Fritillary   *Agraulis vanillae*   Figure 66

Another sun-loving butterfly of the lowlands, common around the coasts of most islands, North and South America. Fiery orange upperside, but distinguished from the Flambeau by the presence of numerous black dots on the forewing and a silver spotted underside. A black caterpillar but with many orange-yellow spots giving a yellow-brown appearance.

Lycaenidae: Blues and Hairstreaks

A vast family of small butterflies distributed worldwide. The shimmering blue colours that many display are structural in nature, being produced by the scales, rather than pigmental. The Hairstreaks

66   Gulf Fritillary, *Agraulis vanillae*

exhibit threadlike tails on the lower wing whilst the Blues have rounded hindwings. The other main subdivision of the Lycaenidae, the Coppers, although common in temperature regions, are largely absent from the West Indies. Flight in this family is fast, irregular and usually short, most species being prone to long periods of settling on leaves with wings together. The stumpy slug-like caterpillars feed on flowers and fruit rather than on foliage. Many lycaenid caterpillars exude a honey-like fluid from between the terminal segments. Ants feed on this secretion and have formed a mutual relationship with the larvae, giving protection from other insect predators and parasites in return for this sweet secretion. At least fifteen species of lycaenid have been recorded from the lesser Antilles and only two representatives are illustrated here (Plates 67 and 68). Most species exhibit this same general body pattern and colouration.

Giant Hairstreak   *Pseudolycaena marsyas*   Figure 68

The largest West Indian Hairstreak with the upperside a shining sky-blue. The underside is silvery with a sprinkling of black dots. Recorded from the Windward Islands, it may often be found in swampy locations.

67   Lycaenid butterfly

68 Giant Hairstreak, *Pseudolycaena marsyas*

Pieridae: Whites and Sulphurs

Small to medium sized butterflies with short or long antennae having well defined or gradually thickened clubs. The best known species are white or yellow, often tinged with black. Found usually in well flowered areas open to the sun. The caterpillars are nearly all green with longitudinal stripes, and smooth, covered at most with very fine short hairs. Favoured food plants are the Cruciferae (Cabbage family), also peas, beans, clovers. The family is represented worldwide.

Great Southern White   *Ascia monuste*   Figure 69

A strongly migratory species common throughout the Caribbean, Southern United States and South America. White with small black, wedge-shaped markings on the outer wing-margins. The other common 'white' of the Caribbean with which this species may be confused is the Florida White, *Appias druscilla* (Figure 70). Here, however, the male has only a suspicion of black at the apex of the forewings whilst the female has a much broader dark brown band around all wing margins.

69   Great Southern White, *Ascia monuste*

70   Florida White, *Appias druscilla*

71 Orange-barred Sulphur,
Phoebis philea

72 Hall's Sulphur, *Eurema leuce*

73 The Gold Rim, *Battus
polydamus*

74 Cattle Heart, *Parides anchises*

Orange-barred Sulphur *Pheobis philea*   Figure 71

About a dozen sulphurs are known from the Lesser Antilles, ranging from white with a dash of yellow through pure lemon yellow and almost to orange. Most smaller sulphurs have a characteristic black triangle at the apex of the forewing, such as the widespread Hall's sulphur, *Eurema leuce* (Figure 72). *Pheobis philea* is representative of the larger sulphurs.

Papilionidae: Swallowtails

The conspicuous tail on the hindwing gives the Swallowtails their popular name. This is a worldwide family of large, conspicuous and dazzlingly beautiful species, particularly numerous in the tropics. Flight in the Swallowtails is swift and can be at great height, though they will come down to drink water from moist sand.

The Gold Rim *Battus polydamas*   Figure 73

Also called the Polydamas Swallowtail or Black Page, this is a widespread species occurring from Southern USA through the Caribbean and South America to Argentina. Each island plays host to a slightly different variation or race, indicating little migration between islands and probable isolation for long periods of time. The basic pattern is black with a submarginal rim of yellow rectangular spots on the lower wing, continuing less prominently on the forewing. The caterpillar is olive-black with a lateral yellowish band at the apex and many fleshy spines or tentacles along the body. The food plant is various kinds of *Aristolochia*, climbing plants.

Cattle Heart *Parides anchises*   Figure 74

A beautiful South American species found in the Caribbean only in Trinidad. Black with red lobes on the hindwing and white dots on the forewing. Closely related to, and often found in the same forested areas as *Parides neophilus* the Spear-winged Cattle Heart, which is distinguished by its more pointed wings. Males of both species have additional greeny blue patches in the central forewing. Caterpillars feed on *Aristolochia*.

Hesperiidae: Skippers

A very large family of stout-bodied short-winged butterflies that resemble day-flying moths. The caterpillars all have large conspicuous heads which appear attached to the body by a narrow 'neck', in reality a small thoracic segment. They are often leaf rollers, living in shelters constructed by drawing leaves together with silken threads and as a consequence are seldom brightly coloured, being predominantly green. The adult butterfly's flight resembles a 'skipping' motion, with forewings closed above the back when settled. Over twenty species of Skipper are known from the Lesser Antilles, many of which are dull brown in colour and not very easy to distinguish. Three common species are illustrated here.

Common Long-tail Skipper *Urbanus proteus* Figure 75

The adult butterfly has the basic brown colouration of the family with irridescent green hair scales on the body and base of the hindwing. Common throughout the West Indies, North and South America this species also has fairly long tails on the hindwing. The caterpillar is yellow-green with a speckled appearance and red head; it feeds on a variety of plants.

The Canna Skipper *Calpodes ethlius* Figure 76

This butterfly is common in gardens where Cannas (on which the larva feeds) are grown. A powerful flier widespread throughout Southern USA, South America and the West Indies with the apparent exception of the Virgin Islands. Upperside is dark brown with numerous white spots; hindwings covered basally in long hair scales.

Tropical Chequered Skipper *Pyrgus oileus* Figure 77

An extremely common butterfly ranging from the Southern USA, through the Caribbean to South America. Chequered colouration of white and brown. Caterpillar is yellow-green, pubescent, with yellow intersegmental membranes and a black head. Feeds on a variety of Malvaceae.

75 Common Long-tail Skipper,
Urbanus proteus

76 Canna Skipper, *Calpodes ethlius*

77 Tropical Chequered Skipper, *Pyrgus oileus*

78   The Monarch, *Danaus plexippus*

79   The Emperor, *Morpho peleides*

Miscellaneous families

The Monarch *Danaus plexippus*   Figure 78

The Danaidae are a cosmopolitan group of robust, broad-winged butterflies, conspicuous and tough, but well protected due to their unpleasant taste. The caterpillars feed on milkweeds and nightshades, plants that have acrid, milky sap from which the protection of both caterpillar and butterfly is derived. The caterpillars are also conspicuous and make no attempt to hide. That of the Monarch is white-yellow with shining black bands and a pair of fleshy tentacles behind the head and near the tail. The adult itself is a rich brown bordered by black wing margins and criss-crossed with heavy black veins. A truly cosmopolitan species occurring in North and South America, Australia and the East Indies. Very strong flier with strong migratory tendencies in temperate regions but not in the tropics where it is usually a solitary flier. Could be confused with *Danaus glippus*, the Queen, although the latter is not as heavily marked with black and is not generally common in the Lesser Antilles.

The Emperor *Morpho peleides*   Figure 79

The family Morphidae (150 species) is exclusive to Tropical Central and South America. Only one species, *Morpho peleides* penetrates the Caribbean into Trinidad and Tobago. This family contains some of the most beautiful butterflies in the world, unmistakable with the large wingspan exhibiting a striking irridescent blue. Males are often found in sunswept gullies where water trickles.

The Cocoa Mort Bleu *Caligo teucer*   Figure 80

The Cocoa Mort Bleu belongs to the family Brassolidae, a group found in well-wooded areas especially at dusk. Blacks, dark browns and sombre blues are the predominant colours. They are well-camouflaged on the underside, bearing a marked resemblance to bark or pieces of wood on which they frequently rest with wings closed. The Cocoa Mort Bleu exhibits a large eye spot on the underside whilst its upperside is a dark midnight blue. It is a South and Central American species, common in the Caribbean only in Trinidad and Tobago, and often found in cocoa estates.

80 The Cocoa Mort Bleu, *Caligo teucer*, front and side views

Euptychia hermes (Satyridae)   Figure 81

A drab brown butterfly with a series of small eyelets on the undersides of the wing; characteristic of the family Satyridae, the Ringlets. This is a large family represented strongly in South and Central America, but generally absent from the Lesser Antilles except for Trinidad and Tobago. Found in shady surroundings, *Euptychia hermes* shows the body pattern and colouration, typical of most of the family, which merges well into the background when the wings are folded at rest. Larvae are generally pale green with stripes and small hairs.

The Blue Transparent *Ithomia pellucida*   Figure 82

This is one of the well-known window pane butterflies (Ithomiidae) of South America which may also be found in Trinidad and Tobago. The wing veins stand out finely in black whilst the wing membrane is otherwise totally transparent like a window pane. In the field, under the darkened shade of the forest, the effect is slightly bluish.

74

81 *Euptychia hermes* (Satyridae)

82 The Blue Transparent, *Ithomia pellucida*

83 Sweet Oil, *Mechanitis isthmia*

Sweet Oil *Mechanitis isthmia* Figure 83

Another South American Ithomid common to Trinidad, but one that is very abundant in shady valleys. A startling obvious colour pattern of black and yellow blotches on a light brown ground colour. These are warning colours advertising bad taste to predators. Two other rarer *Mechanitis* species utilise the same basic colour patterns, a phenomenon known as Mullerian mimicry, after its discoverer F. Müller in 1879. Here similar distasteful species use the same basic warning colours to reinforce the design. A similar phenomenon is exhibited in the black and yellow stripes of many wasps. The Sweet Oil is also mimicked in Trinidad by the Isabella Tiger, *Eneides isabella*, a palatable species which is afforded protection by its distasteful models. This habit is termed Batesian mimicry, after the famous naturalist H.W. Bates who spent much time in the Amazon basin and drew attention to this phenomenon in 1861. Models and mimics are of course active in the same habitats but it is important that the mimic does not become too common or its protection will be lost.

84 The Tiger, *Tithorea harmonia*

The Tiger   *Tithorea harmonia*   Figure 84

Exhibiting black, yellow and brown colours common to many
ithomids, this Trinidadian species is common in the shaded semi-
forested areas and cocoa estates.

Giant Silkworm moth   Saturnidae   Figures 85 and 86

There are many species of saturnid moths that come to lights at night.
Giant Silkworms are amongst the largest and most beautiful of moths,
often being brightly coloured with large eyespots on the wings. The
antennae of the males are large and feathery. The caterpillars are large,
armed with spines and feed largely on the foliage of trees, whilst the
adults are short-lived and never feed. Although the caterpillars spin
tough cocoons, attempts to utilise the silk commercially, as in the true
Asiatic Silkworm, have been unsuccessful.

85 *Citheronia magnifica* (Saturnidae)

86 *Automeris metzli* (Saturnidae)

87 *Xylophanes titana* (Sphingidae)   **88** *Agrius cingulatus* (Sphingidae)

Sphinx moth Sphingidae   Figures 87 and 88

The Sphinx or hawk moths have stiff, powerful wings that are often boldly or colourfully patterned. Their wings beat so rapidly that some day-flying species can be mistaken for hummingbirds. Many adults visit flowers for nectar and have long proboscos that are coiled under the head when not in use. Strongly attracted to artificial light.

10 Class Arachnida: Spiders and scorpions

Arachnids differ from insects in lacking antennae and wings and in having eight rather than six legs. With over 75 000 species worldwide, they comprise the largest non-insect class of arthropod animals. Arachnids, which first appeared at least 350 million years ago, also differ from insects having fang-bearing appendages, called chelicereae, in front of the mouth. The body is generally in two distinct parts, a cephalothorax (combined head and thorax) and an abdomen. There are usually six finger-like silk glands, called spinnerets, located beneath the abdomen just in front of the anus. Not all spiders spin webs. Some live in burrows which they line with silk, whilst others have no retreat at all. The eggs are laid in silken sacs and the young, called spiderlings, resemble adults and are cannibalistic. Legs lost during development can be regenerated. Although spiders do not have wings, small ones can 'fly' by spinning out some silk which catches the wind.

Included in this class are the mites and ticks (order Acarina), the daddy-long-legs (order Opiliones), the scorpions (Scorpionida) and related whipscorpions, pseudoscorpions, windscorpions or camel spiders, and of course the spiders. Only the common spiders and a scorpion are considered here.

Spiders are voracious predators which use venom to paralyse or kill insect prey or, more rarely, vertebrates. Few spiders bite people, however, and the venom of most is harmless. Legends persist, hence the recommendation to dance the tarantella as a remedy for bites by the European tarantula.

Tarantula or Bird-eating spider   Theraphosidae   Figure 89

Tarantulas are large, hairy spiders, 35 mm or more long, with a leg span of up to 150 mm. Although greatly feared as being fatally poisonous the bite, though painful, is no more dangerous than a bee sting in most species. More troublesome are the abdominal bristles which break off easily and can irritate the skin. Nocturnal, tarantulas hide in dark cavities or burrows during the day venturing out to forage at night. They do not spin webs, although the burrow is usually lined with silk, but pounce on their prey. On an insect diet of moths and grasshoppers plus a little water, theraphosid spiders can live in captivity for a period of 10-25 years. They are called 'bird-eating' because of their rare habit of taking young birds from the nest. They are also called banana spiders, arriving in temperate parts with cargoes of fruit.

Orb Weaver Arnaeidae   Figure 90

Amongst the web building spiders, orb weavers are prominent both in terms of number and in design of web. Orb weavers spin spiralling orb webs on support lines that radiate outwards from the centre. The plane of the web may be vertical, horizontal or slanting. Many replace the entire web daily, spinning a new web in the early evening in about an hour. Though spiral strands of the web are covered in viscous sticky material, the radiating strands are simple silk. In the centre, on a dense net of silk, lies the spider. Different species exhibit different

89 Tarantula   **90** Orb Weaver

91 Golden Silk spider,
   Nephila clavipes

92 Wolf spider

93 Jumping spider

94 Scorpion

variations in web design. The male usually spins its own web in an outlying portion of the female's web. As in most spider groups, the female is much larger than the male. Mating is sometimes preceded by an elaborate courtship performance and often followed by the female killing and eating the male. (Hence the name 'Black Widow' for one species of spider.)

Golden Silk spider   *Nephila clavipes*   Figure 91

Amongst the orb weavers, the golden silk spider is probably the most distinctive. Ranging from the Southern USA into the tropics, these spiders are aptly named on account of the large amount and strength of their silk, which is sometimes used in the manufacture of fabrics. The webs spun are the biggest of any in the world, frequently measuring two or three metres across.

Wolf spider   Lycosidae   Figure 92

The lycosids are aptly named after the Greek word *'lycosa'* meaning wolf. Moderate to large spiders, they live on the ground and actively pursue their prey at night. Since they do not spin webs, the egg sac is carried along by the female, attached to her spinnerets. The spiderlings too may be carried about on the female's back until they are ready to disperse.

Jumping spider   Salticidae   Figure 93

This large family gets its name from the spectacular leaps the spiders make pouncing on prey. Generally small spiders of black and white or metallic green appearance, some are also ant-mimics. They commonly enter dwellings, hunting on widowsills or walls where small moths are attracted by lights.

Scorpion   Scorpionida   Figure 94

Scorpions are well known arachnids varying in length up to about 130 mm. Lobster-like in appearance with large, claw-like pedipalps but with an upturned stinger on the end of the abdomen. The scorpion's sting has long been feared (hence the position as a Zodiac sign), but although painful, stings are not usually lethal. Scorpions are nocturnal, killing spiders and large insects. Females give birth to live young which ride on the mother's back until the first moult. They mature slowly, taking as long as five years to become adult.

11 Class Diplopoda: Millipedes

Figure 95

The millipedes are elongate wormlike animals with many legs, most having over 30 pairs and bearing two pairs on each body segment. They frequent damp places such as rotting wood, soil or humus. Millipedes do not bite but some are able to give off an ill-smelling fluid which can be strong enough to kill insects that are placed in a jar with the millipede. The fluid may contain hydrogen cyanide and explode on contact with the air. This is strictly a defensive reaction for millipedes are not generally predaceous but feed on plant material, live or decaying.

95 Millipede

12 Class Chilopoda: Centipedes

Figure 96

The distinction between the centipedes and the millipedes is in the number of legs, centipedes having only one pair per segment. Both occur in the same habitats but centipedes are predaceous and are fast running and more active. Insects and spiders make up the largest part of the diet. All centipedes possess poison jaws which they use to paralyse their prey. Smaller varieties are quite harmless but some larger tropical types such as *Scolopendra dromorpha* (Plate 96) can reach a foot in length (30 cm) and give a nasty bite.

96 Centipede